Insect
Adaptations

Mouthparts, Mimicry, and Flying

Andi Diehn

Illustrated by Lex Cornell

EXPLORE MORE PICTURE BOOK ADAPTATIONS!

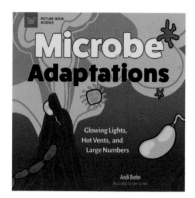
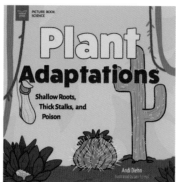

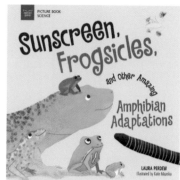

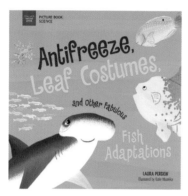
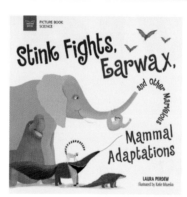
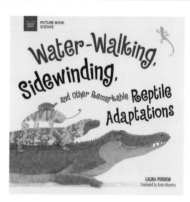

Check out more titles at www.nomadpress.net

Nomad Press

A division of Nomad Communications

10 9 8 7 6 5 4 3 2 1

This book was manufactured by
CGB Printers North Mankato, Minnesota
November 2024, Job #1082658

ISBN Softcover: 978-1-64741-131-2
ISBN Hardcover: 978-1-64741-128-2

Educational Consultant, Marla Conn

Questions regarding the ordering of this book should be addressed to
Nomad Press
PO Box 1036, Norwich, VT 05055
www.nomadpress.net

Printed in the United States.

SPRINGING! FLYING! MUNCHING! HIDING!
Insects are everywhere,
but they can be easy to miss.

THEY'RE MASTERS OF DISGUISE,
Shapes and colors blending
into their environment.

THEY'RE FAST,
Moving on quick legs and
whizzing through the air.

THEY'RE SMALL,
Folding tiny bodies into
cracks and crevices.

THEY'RE MANY,
Outnumbering humans
and all other species.

**WHAT KINDS OF INSECTS
ARE CRAWLING AROUND YOU RIGHT NOW?**

Have you ever seen a grasshopper
jumping up from tall grass?

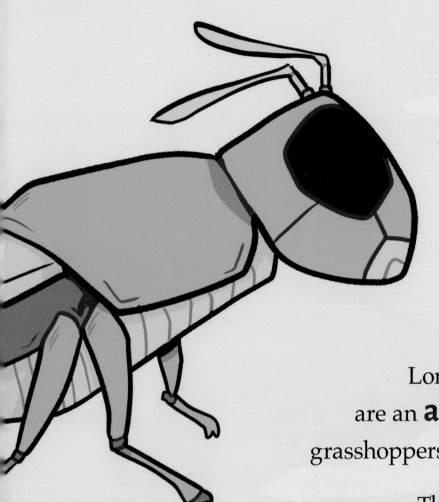

Those must be some
pretty strong
jumping
legs!

Long, springlike legs
are an **adaptation** that helps
grasshoppers survive in their **habitat.**

Those legs let them
leap away from danger or take off in flight.

Adaptation means fitting into an **environment** to survive. For example, some insects have wings so they can fly around. Others have strong jaws to chew their food.

Insects with traits that help them survive live long enough to pass down these **characteristics** to their offspring.

SLOWER

BIG JUMPS

FAST

SMALL WINGS

LOW JUMPS

Because the offspring have the same characteristics as their parents, they are the ones to survive.

As time passes, the characteristics that don't help with survival appear less and less often.

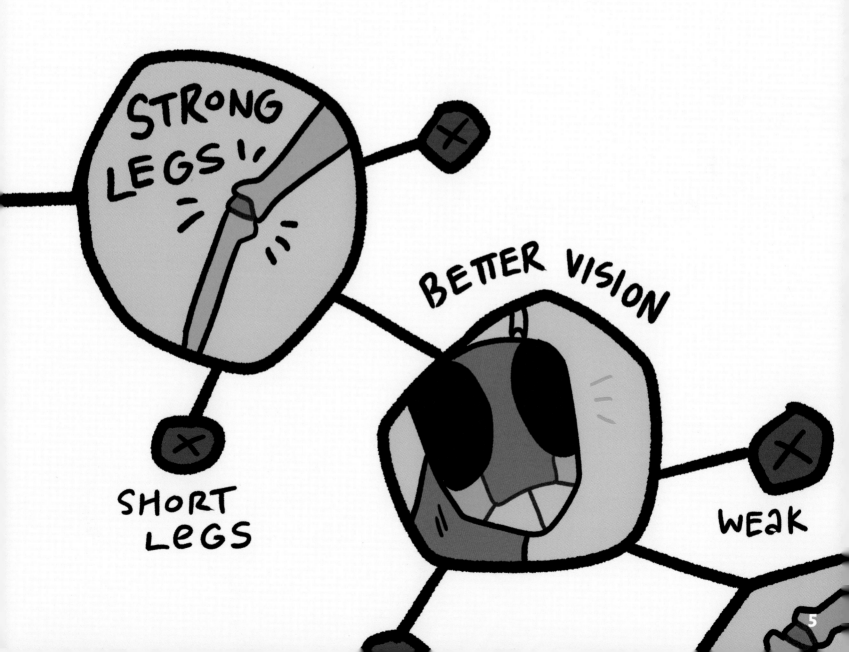

STRONG LEGS

SHORT LEGS

BETTER VISION

WEAK

Mimicry is another adaptation
we can see in the insect world.

The **giant swallowtail caterpillar**
hangs out on the **tops of leaves**, but it is
not green like many other caterpillars that
use camouflage to hide from predators.

The giant swallowtail caterpillar is **WHITE** and **BLACK,** but lots of **predators** avoid it because it looks like . . .

What do frogs order when they go to a restaurant?

....

FRENCH FLIES!

You can bet that predators such as wasps and flies aren't going near that!

While the giant swallowtail caterpillar looks like a yucky substance to help it avoid getting eaten, the stick insect does the opposite.

It has adapted to look like
its surroundings—sticks!

Stick insects—also called walking sticks—
are GRAYISH BROWN in color.

Their bodies and legs are long and twiggy.
Some kinds of stick insects even walk with a swaying
motion that mimics a stick being blown in a breeze.

Stick insects adapted to their
woody environments by adopting
a shape and color that helps **camouflage**
them from predators.

Can you spot the stick insects in this picture?

Who comes to a picnic
but is never invited?
....
ANTS!

You can also see adaptation at work when you take a closer look at how certain insects eat.

Butterflies have a looooong mouthpart called a **proboscis.** It's perfect for sucking up nectar, water, and juice from flowers and fruits.

When they're hungry, butterflies stick out their **proboscis,** have a yummy liquid meal, and then curl the proboscis back on their faces.

What did the dog say to the flea?
······································
STOP BUGGING ME!

That's a very different way of eating
than the way beetles eat.

Beetles have mouthparts called **mandibles**
that are perfect for chewing.

Mandibles move sideways,
crushing up leaves, roots, and seeds.

**Some insects have
more than one kind
of mouthpart!**

MANDIBLES

PROBOSCIS

**Honeybees have a
probiscis for sucking up
nectar and mandibles
for chewing pollen.**

Insects are pretty small, right?

Even the ones that seem huge,
such as the **white witch moth,** are
tiny compared to most other animals.

WHITE WITCH MOTH

MONARCH BUTTERFLY

One tool some insects use to increase their chances of survival is **flight.**

Have you ever had a mosquito land on you or watched a lightning bug flash around at night or noticed a dragonfly come to rest on a long piece of grass?

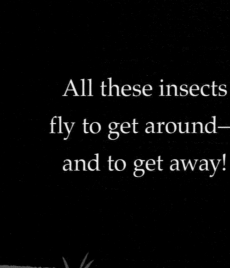

All these insects fly to get around— and to get away!

What do you call a nervous beetle?

··

A JITTER-BUG!

Insects have developed wings that let them zip away from predators, zoom around in search of something to eat, and explore their surroundings to find places to rest.

GREEN MOSS
PEACOCK BUTTERFLY

LUNA
MOTH

ATLAS
MOTH

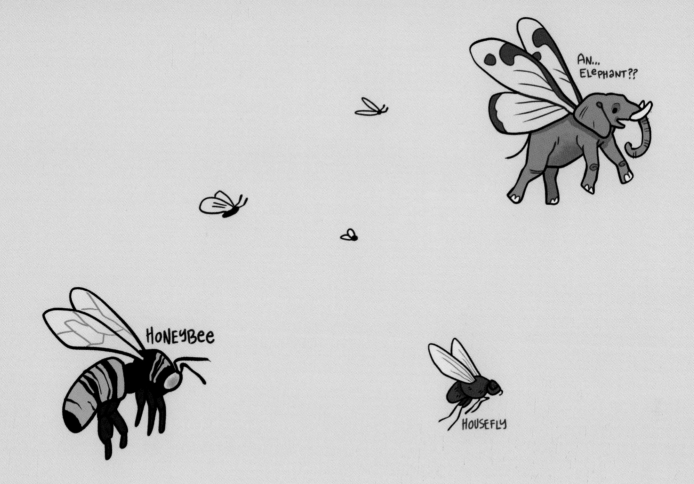

And it's not just wings that are necessary for flight.

A small, lightweight body is essential! Maybe that's why you don't see a whole lot of elephants flying across the sky! They would need enormous wings to carry all that weight.

Living creatures adapt
so they can
eat,
drink,
avoid being eaten,
and **reproduce.**

How does adaptation help insects with reproduction?

One way many kinds of **insects have adapted**
is by having lots of babies.

The African driver ant can
lay 3 to 4 million eggs
every 25 days!

Even if many
of the eggs
don't survive,
there will
still be lots
of babies.

These African driver ants travel in armies of
millions along the
forest floor and eat everything
in their path, including
snakes,
birds, and
other animals.

They work together to get jobs done!

Why did the queen bee go to the doctor?

SHE HAD HIVES!

Hey!

That's another adaptation, one that people share.

Many insect colonies work together to do greater things than any one individual can accomplish.

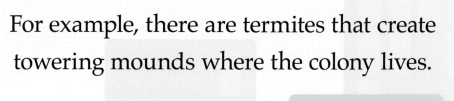

For example, there are termites that create towering mounds where the colony lives.

People build towns and cities where they live, work, and play, just as termites build their mounds.

What do you call a beetle that's bad at football?

....

A FUMBLE-BEE!

All around the world, insects are adapting to changes in their environments. As the **climate** changes and different areas **warm up** or **cool down,** insects are figuring out how to survive and thrive!

What are some
adaptations
you notice in
the insects
around you?

Eat Your Snack With a Proboscis!

What You Need

several plates - one straw for every person -
water - Jell-o or pudding - cereal - crackers -
berries - other snack foods

What You Do

- Place the water and foods onto separate plates.

- Each scientist gets their own straw.

- Try using your straw to eat the crackers. What happens?

- Use your straw to eat the berries. What happens?

- Use the straw to drink the water. What happens?

- Try eating all the different kinds of food with your straw.

- Use a spoon to eat the parts of your snack
  that didn't fit in your straw!

Think About It! Which food is easiest to suck up
into your mouth? Why? What does this show
you about the different ways insects eat?

Fruit flies were the first living creatures to be sent into space.

Houseflies have feet that are about 10 million times more sensitive than human tongues.

Grasshoppers existed before dinosaurs!

About 1.5 million different insect species have been named around the world.

Ants can carry more than 50 times their own weight.

Some species of moth can live underwater for weeks without coming up for air, making them the first-known amphibious insects.

A bee might fly up to 60 miles in one day as it gathers food.

Some insects replace their body water with a chemical called glycerol that keeps their bodies from freezing during cold months.

Mosquitoes are attracted to smelly feet!

Glossary

adaptation: a change that a living thing makes to become better suited to its environment.

amphibious: living or able to live both on land and in water.

camouflage: the colors or patterns that allow a plant or animal to blend in with its environment.

characteristic: a feature or quality.

climate: the weather patterns in an area during a long period of time.

environment: the area in which something lives.

habitat: the natural area where a plant or animal lives.

insect: an animal that has three body parts and six legs and its skeleton on the outside of its body. Many insects have wings. Grasshoppers, ants, ladybugs, and honeybees are all insects.

mandible: in some insects, a strong biting mouthpart.

mimicry: looking like or acting like something else.

offspring: the young of a plant, insect, or animal.

predator: an animal that hunts and eats other animals.

proboscis: the sucking mouthpart of insects such as butterflies and bees.

reproduce: to produce offspring.

species: a group of plants or animals that are closely related and produce offspring.

trait: a characteristic.